MOLES
Champion Excavators

by Eulalia García
Illustrated by Gabriel Casadevall and Ali Garousi

Gareth Stevens Publishing
MILWAUKEE

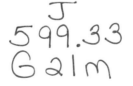

For a free color catalog describing Gareth Stevens' list of high-quality books and multimedia programs, call 1-800-542-2595 (USA) or 1-800-461-9120 (Canada). Gareth Stevens Publishing's Fax: (414) 225-0377.
See our catalog, too, on the World Wide Web: http://gsinc.com

The editor would like to extend special thanks to Jan W. Rafert, Curator of Primates and Small Mammals, Milwaukee County Zoo, Milwaukee, Wisconsin, for his kind and professional help with the information in this book.

Library of Congress Cataloging-in-Publication Data

García, Eulalia.
  [Topo. English]
  Moles: champion excavators / by Eulalia García ; illustrated by Gabriel Casadevall and Ali Garousi.
    p. cm. – (Secrets of the animal world)
  Includes bibliographical references and index.
  Summary: Describes the physical characteristics and habits of moles, animals known for their ability to dig.
  ISBN 0-8368-1646-3 (lib. bdg.)
  1. Moles (Animals)–Juvenile literature. [1. Moles (Animals).] I. Casadevall, Gabriel, ill. II. Garousi, Ali, ill. III. Title. IV. Series.
QL737.I57G3713 1997
599.33'5–dc21   97-8487

This North American edition first published in 1997 by
Gareth Stevens Publishing
1555 North RiverCenter Drive, Suite 201
Milwaukee, Wisconsin 53212 USA

This U.S. edition © 1997 by Gareth Stevens, Inc. Created with original © 1993 Ediciones Este, S.A., Barcelona, Spain. Additional end matter © 1997 by Gareth Stevens, Inc.

Series editor: Patricia Lantier-Sampon
Editorial assistants: Diane Laska, Rita Reitci

Printed in the United States of America

1 2 3 4 5 6 7 8 9 01 00 99 98 97

CONTENTS

BUILDERS OF TUNNELS

Where moles live

Moles are small, insectivorous mammals. The most abundant species is the common mole, which lives in open areas such as fields, gardens, and parks, mostly in Europe and Asia. The golden mole lives in southern Africa and has copper-colored fur. The most unusual species is the star-nosed mole. Its snout has twenty-two thin feelers.

The common mole is about 6 inches (15 centimeters) long. Males weigh about 4 ounces (110 grams). Females weigh about 3 ounces (85 g).

Moles lead secretive lives in Europe, Asia, Japan, North America, and some areas of Africa.

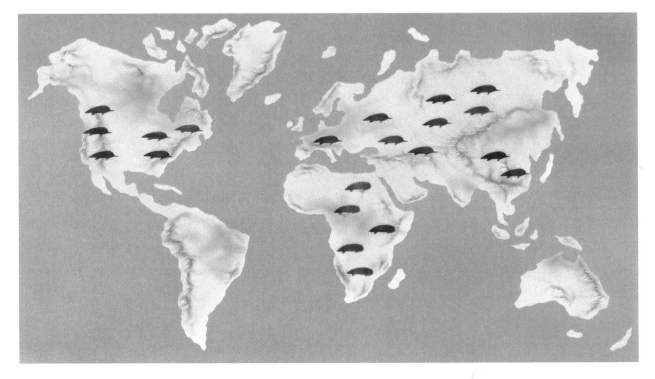

Invisible neighbors

Few animals live entirely underground as moles do. If not for mole hills, these small mammals would hardly ever be noticed. Moles leave the tunnels only if food is scarce underground. They eat worms inside their tunnels, but they may go out to catch lizards, mice, and birds. They may also come out to search for water. Each mole excavates its own tunnel system, some of which are pathways that can be used by other animals.

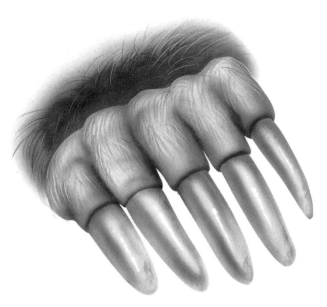

The paws of moles make useful tools for digging soil. They are large with long nails and are covered with fur.

The common mole made the hills in this field. Beneath the hills lie tunnel systems. The den is in the largest hill.

Underground engineers

Many species of digging animals exist, but only a few live entirely underground: some marsupials, a few rodents, and moles. These animals have similar features: an oval shape, plush fur, small eyes and ears, and a specially developed body part for digging. Mole species include, among others, common moles, star-nosed moles, and golden moles.

Moles and worm snakes spend their lives underground. Other diggers, such as marmots and platypuses, construct only underground nests.

MARMOT

GOLDEN MOLE

COMMON MOLE

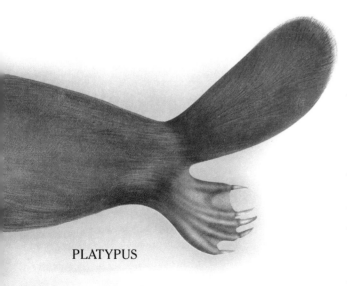

STAR-NOSED MOLE

PLATYPUS

Some mammals dig underground dens for shelter from the weather, to hide from enemies, to sleep, or to bring up their young. Marmots, for example, live in groups of up to twelve individuals that take refuge in a deep den for the winter. When they come out to search for food, a guard stays behind to warn the rest of any danger.

Platypuses construct underground dwellings with an underwater entrance. They eat fish, aquatic insects, and mollusks, which they find by digging.

Worm snakes dig tunnels and penetrate ant and termite nests to eat the larvae.

INSIDE THE MOLE

All moles are adapted to life underground, but the star-nosed mole is also aquatic. It builds its den in moist soil with an exit under water. The star-nosed mole is about 4 inches (10 cm) long and weighs about 1.5-3 ounces (40-80 g). It is an expert swimmer that eats small fish, crustaceans, aquatic insects, and worms. The star-nosed mole is not as solitary as the common mole and prefers to live in small groups.

FUR
The mole's fur does not grow toward the back, as in most mammals, but in all directions. This helps the animal go forward and backward easily inside the tunnels.

BODY
The mole's compact body shape is ideal for running through narrow tunnels.

LIVER

KIDNEY

INTESTINE

FEMUR

TAIL
The tail of common moles has a sense of touch, and the animals carry it up in the air. The tail of the star-nosed mole is a fat reserve for winter.

STOMACH

BLADDER

FEET
The feet hold on to the sides of the tunnel when the mole digs into the soil.

SKIN
The mole's skin is thick. The animal's weight is on the skin-covered chest when it is digging or resting.

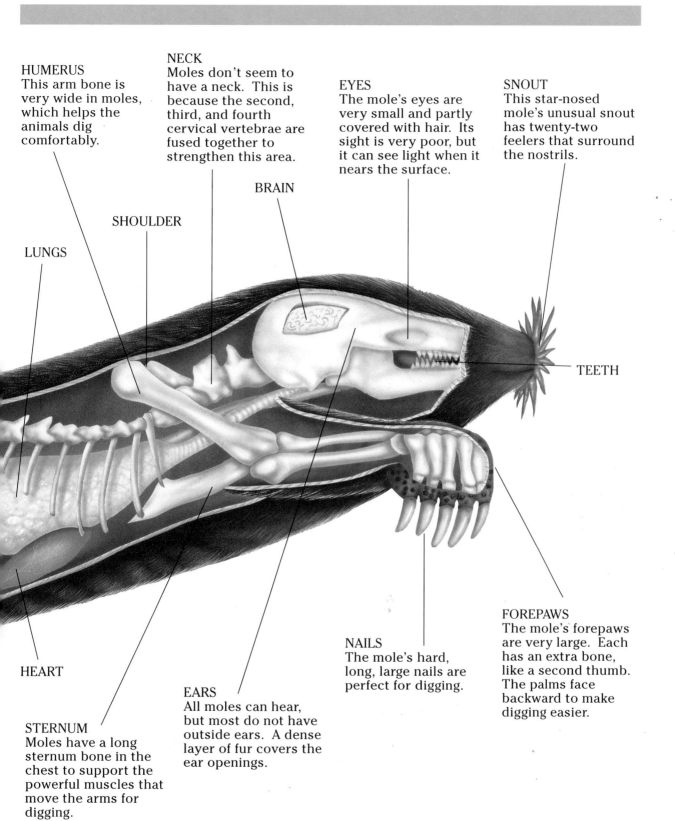

HUMERUS
This arm bone is very wide in moles, which helps the animals dig comfortably.

NECK
Moles don't seem to have a neck. This is because the second, third, and fourth cervical vertebrae are fused together to strengthen this area.

EYES
The mole's eyes are very small and partly covered with hair. Its sight is very poor, but it can see light when it nears the surface.

SNOUT
This star-nosed mole's unusual snout has twenty-two feelers that surround the nostrils.

BRAIN

SHOULDER

LUNGS

TEETH

HEART

EARS
All moles can hear, but most do not have outside ears. A dense layer of fur covers the ear openings.

NAILS
The mole's hard, long, large nails are perfect for digging.

FOREPAWS
The mole's forepaws are very large. Each has an extra bone, like a second thumb. The palms face backward to make digging easier.

STERNUM
Moles have a long sternum bone in the chest to support the powerful muscles that move the arms for digging.

EXPERT MINERS

Master excavators

The mole is a master digger. Its dwelling is a complicated system of tunnels over 330 feet (100 m) in length and 3 feet (1 m) deep. There are three types of tunnels. Some are for traveling around, and others are excavated in spring for mating. Both of these types of tunnels can be found close to the surface. The third type are deep hunting tunnels

Moles dig for four hours and rest for three and a half hours. This cycle is repeated three times a day.

The mole's dwelling consists of tunnels surrounding the den, hunting tunnels, and the pantry.

MOLE HILL

NEST

PANTRY

When worms are plentiful, the mole stores them in its pantry. As many as 1,200 worms have been found in a single room.

TRANSVERSE TUNNEL

that lead to the outside through mole hills. Tunnels are oval in shape and measure 2 inches (5 cm) wide by 1.6 inches (4 cm) high. The mole enters or leaves its den through the mole hill, closing up the hole after itself.

Both sexes dig tunnels, but the male's tunnels are longer and straighter.

All tunnel systems have a large room carpeted with grass. This is the den, or refuge, and it lies underneath a very big mound of exterior soil.

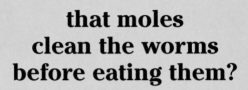

that moles clean the worms before eating them?

Worms eat and dig at the same time because they pass the earth through their digestive tract. Their bodies extract the food they need and excrete the rest.

Moles are careful not to swallow earth when they dig. When they capture a worm, they clean it before eating it by passing it through their forepaws.

Some moles may have venomous saliva that paralyzes the prey before eating or storing them.

UNDERGROUND PASSAGES

Hunting in the tunnels

Moles die if they go more than twelve hours without eating. Since their diet has lots of water but not much protein or fat, they have to eat more than humans do. A mole can devour three times its own weight in worms every day.

Moles dig tunnels to hunt animals that live in the earth. When worms and other invertebrates come through the soil and fall into the tunnel, a patrolling mole will soon detect the prey. When the soil has little prey, moles dig longer tunnels to obtain more food.

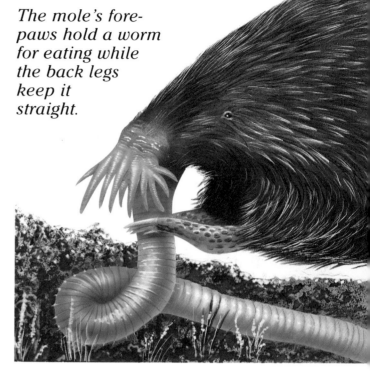

The mole's fore-paws hold a worm for eating while the back legs keep it straight.

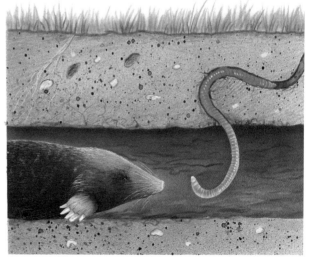

The tunnels collect food for the mole. With its acute hearing and sharp sense of smell, the mole detects the worm before it can find its way out.

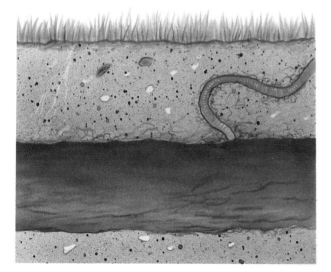

With a pick and a shovel

Moles are excellent diggers
because they have two useful
tools in each hand — a pick and
a shovel. When they dig shallow
tunnels, they use only one
forepaw. The mole lifts the earth
it digs out and presses it against
the ceiling, forming an outside
ridge. Deep tunnels are also
excavated with just one forepaw.
From time to time, the mole
turns around and pushes the
piled-up soil toward the outside
with the other hand to form a
hill, or it pushes the soil into
an unused tunnel.

*When digging deep tunnels, moles
push the earth to the surface.*

*The hills and
ridges of dirt in
this field are
shallow tunnels
dug by a
common mole.*

that moles have a
good sense of direction?

Like other animal species, moles establish their own territories. Surprisingly, they do not get lost in the dark tunnels. They have an acute sense of direction and can detect vibrations in the soil. Moles never stop exploring the soil of their tunnels with their snout and whiskers. They go through their tunnels, repairing cave-ins and keeping the walls in good shape.

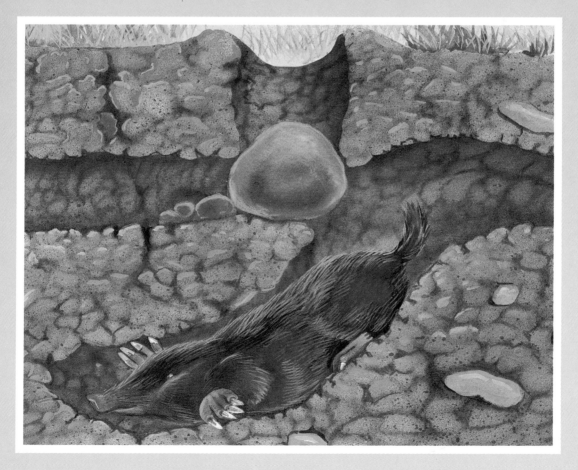

Golden moles and sausages

Golden moles are insectivorous but belong to a different family than do the common mole and the star-nosed mole. They have a cylindrical body and short limbs. The front limbs have two or three very strong nails for digging. Golden moles excavate at a depth of 3 feet (1 m) and can dig down in a spiral more than 650 feet (200 m) in length.

Golden moles feed in the upper tunnels, while in the deeper ones they build their nests, the refuge, and the room for their wastes.

When a snake enters the den of naked mole-rats, the mole-rats block the tunnels with dirt by digging quickly with their hind legs.

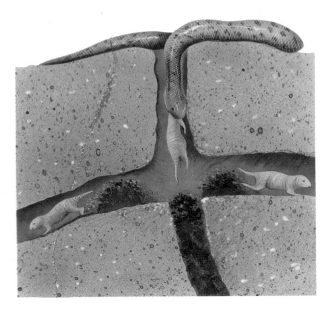

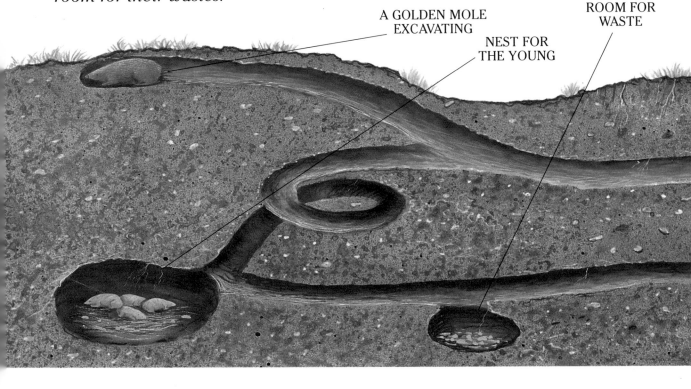

A GOLDEN MOLE
EXCAVATING

NEST FOR
THE YOUNG

ROOM FOR
WASTE

Other expert diggers not related to moles are the naked mole-rats. They have naked, hairless bodies and huge teeth. Because of their appearance, these rodents have nicknames like "baby walrus" or "sausages with saber teeth."

Naked mole-rats excavate in teams. The animals of a colony stand in line behind the one that is digging with its teeth. The second one picks up the dirt and sweeps it with its feet to the surface. Near the exit, another

The "baby walrus" feed on roots they find when digging their tunnels.

mole-rat passes the load to a large companion that stands at the end of the line. This "muscle man" is in charge of moving the dirt as fast as it can.

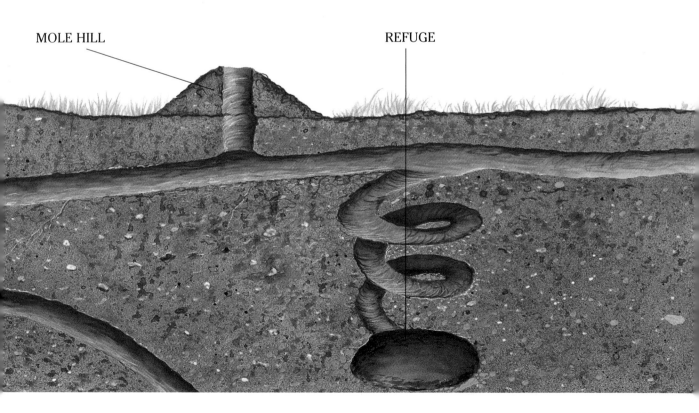

MOLE HILL

REFUGE

THE FIRST INSECTIVORES

Mole history

Mammals are animals that have evolved different ways of living in many kinds of habitats. Mammals can swim, climb, leap, fly, run, and dig. Primitive insectivores were the mammals from which all of today's mammals have descended.

The first insectivores lived about 100 million years ago when dinosaurs still dominated Earth. These insectivores included many different types of animals, who, although not closely related, shared similar

Marsupial moles (above) and golden moles are examples of convergent evolution. They evolved separately, yet they look very similar.

The first mammals were insectivores, many of which lived in trees.

characteristics because they adapted to the same type of life. This type of evolution is called convergent evolution.

Convergent evolution also took place in marsupials. For example, the marsupial mole's fur and forepaws look a lot like those of the golden mole, and both have skin-covered eyes. Digging habits also developed in marsupials. The necrolest, which means "tomb thief," was a marsupial in South America 25 million years ago.

The necrolest had a snout that resembled an open flower, similar to the star-nosed mole's snout. Like the mole, the necrolest's sense of touch was in the snout, and the animal used its snout to find its food.

Did You Know...?

that moles
are very aggressive?

The common mole lives alone, although in areas with plenty of worms it can share parts of its tunnel systems. Males and females remain together only for a few hours to mate. Moles try to avoid entering each other's tunnels. If an invasion occurs, they fight until the stronger mole wins.

When a tunnel system loses its builder, other moles hurry to invade it. Some moles claim territory by leaving scent marks.

THE MOLE'S BEHAVIOR

Born underground

Moles lose their aggressiveness only during the mating season. At this time, a male can enter the female's den to mate. Between 28 to 42 days after mating, the female gives birth to three to seven young in a special room lined with branches and leaves.

The young are born without hair. They are pink and blind and weigh only 0.1 ounce (3 g). They feed on mother's milk for one month. They remain with her five or six weeks after birth.

Moles are born naked and blind. At three weeks, they open their eyes and weigh more than 2 ounces (60 g).

In spring, female moles allow males into their territory.

The good and the bad

Moles can destroy gardens, fields, and crops with their tunnels. Horticulturists say underground digging by moles destroys tree roots and plants.

Burrowing moles aerate the soil, so the animals can actually help plants grow in a better soil environment. Moles also eat larvae and insects that are harmful to crops.

Much of the damage blamed on moles is really caused by the actions of digging rodents, which feed on tubers and roots.

Moles do not eat the roots and bulbs of trees and plants, but field mice do.

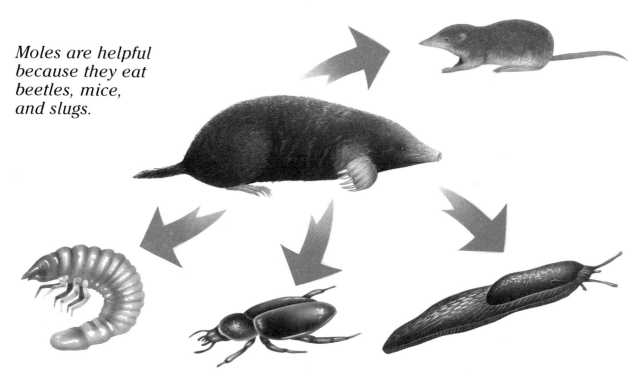

Moles are helpful because they eat beetles, mice, and slugs.

Unwelcome visitors

In its underground tunnels, the mole has few enemies, although snakes and badgers sometimes enter the tunnels.

The mole gives off an odor that makes it repulsive to many carnivores, but weasels, foxes, martens, and birds of prey still hunt it. When it goes outside and is surprised by an enemy, it rarely escapes because it is very clumsy when it walks.

Moles have many enemies outside their tunnels, such as porcupines.

The mole and its young can be surprised in their home by a badger.

APPENDIX TO

SECRETS
OF THE
ANIMAL WORLD

MOLES
Champion Excavators

MOLE SECRETS

▼ **Mole cricket.** This insect, like the mole, has powerful front legs for digging tunnels. As it moves forward, it chews roots with its strong jaws.

▼ **Making its own bed.** Pangolins are scaly mammals that eat termites. They dig underground tunnels to sleep in during the day.

Noisy moles. When moles are excited, they make a grumbling sound. They also scream inside their tunnels and make chewing and breathing noises as they explore.

▼ **Safe from the heat.** Gerbils and kangaroo rats live in deserts, where they dig dens with their teeth. During the day they remain in their dens, protected from the sun.

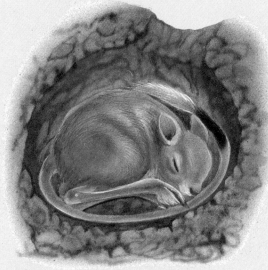

Colored moles. Mole fur is normally black, but it can also be gray, cream colored, orangy rose, or even completely white.

Good swimmers. All moles, not only the star-nosed mole, are good swimmers. This ability comes in handy when the dens are flooded by rain. If this happens frequently, moles then begin to lead nomadic lives, moving often from one place to another.

▶ **After the mole's trail.** Moles leave unmistakable trails. As they walk, they leave the nail prints of each forepaw. Since the forepaws point backward, they don't rest on the ground. In soft soil, the hind feet and the body also leave marks.

1. Where does the golden mole live?
a) In Japan.
b) In North America.
c) In southern Africa.

2. What indicates the presence of moles?
a) Their excrement.
b) The mole hills on the ground's surface.
c) The chewed trunks of the trees.

3. What do naked mole-rats use to dig the earth?
a) Their nails.
b) Their tail.
c) Their teeth.
d) Their feet.

4. When are moles not aggressive?
a) During the mating season.
b) Inside their tunnels.
c) When they go outside the tunnels.

5. How are moles beneficial?
a) They aerate the ground and feed on harmful insect larvae.
b) They eat roots and weeds.
c) They flatten crop fields.

6. How many feelers does the star-nosed mole snout have?
a) Fifteen.
b) Twenty-two.
c) Ten.
d) Seventeen.

The answers to MOLE SECRETS questions are on page 32.

GLOSSARY

acute: sharp; intense.

adapt: to change behavior or adjust needs in order to survive in changing conditions.

aerate: to supply or mix air into.

aggressive: bold; eager to challenge or engage in combat.

aquatic: living or growing in water.

carnivores: animals that eat primarily meat.

cervical vertebrae: small, interconnected bone segments of the spinal column that make up the neck.

characteristics: traits or features that separate one object or organism from another.

colony: a community with members that live and work together.

convergent evolution: the development, in different and unrelated animals or plants, of structures or functions that are similar.

crustaceans: animals with a hard outer shell that live mostly in water. Snails are crustaceans that live on land.

cylindrical: shaped like a cylinder; like a tube or pipe.

descended: to have evolved from particular ancestors or previous generations.

devour: to eat hungrily or greedily.

digestive tract: the internal passageway of an animal that passes food through the body, where it breaks down into nourishing particles. The body uses what it needs and sends the remainder out as waste.

dominate: to have the greatest influence; the animals or plants in greatest numbers in a region are said to dominate their environment.

dwelling: a shelter in which animals or humans live.

engineers: designers and builders of engines, bridges, roads, tunnels, and other similar structures.

establish: to bring something about; to start something.

evolve: to change or develop gradually from one form to another. All living things change and adapt to survive or they may become extinct.

excavate: to dig out and remove.

excrete: to send out as waste.

exterior: the outer surface.

extract: to take what is needed from something.

fused: to be blended together; in animals, separate structures that evolved to become one piece, such as neck bones.

habitat: the natural home of a plant or animal.

habits: the behavior patterns of animals.

horticulturist: a scientist who specializes in growing fruits, vegetables, and flowers.

insectivorous: the habit of eating mainly insects.

invade: to enter by force or without permission.

invertebrates: animals that do not have a backbone or spinal cord.

larva (*pl* larvae): the wingless, wormlike form of a newly-hatched insect; in the life cycle of insects, amphibians, and some other organisms, the stage that comes after the egg but before full development.

mammals: warm-blooded animals that have backbones and hair. Female mammals produce milk to feed their young.

marsupials: animals similar to the kangaroo that have a pouch for carrying the young.

mate (*v*): to join together (animals) to produce young.

mollusks: a large group of invertebrate animals with a soft body enclosed in a shell, such as snails and clams.

nomadic: having no fixed dwelling; traveling from place to place.

pantry: a place where food is stored.

penetrate: to pass into or through something.

prey: animals that are hunted, captured, and killed for food by other animals.

refuge: a place of safety; a shelter.

repulsive: arousing disgust.

rodents: a group of mammals with large front teeth for gnawing. Beavers, mice, rats, and squirrels are rodents.

shallow: not very deep.

solitary: living alone; isolated.

species: animals or plants that are closely related and often similar in behavior and appearance. Members of the same species are capable of breeding together.

territory: an area occupied by one or several of the same kind of animal. Animals forage for food and build nests or other shelters in their territories.

venomous: poisonous.

vibrations: quivering or trembling motions. Moles can sense the location of any animal that enters their tunnels by the vibrations it makes in the earth.

ACTIVITIES

◆ Besides moles, many other kinds of animals also live underground. Visit a library for books that tell about some of these other animals and where they live. Try to find animals in various climates, such as deserts, tropics, or temperate areas. Do they live underground for the same or for different reasons, such as escaping heat? See if you can identify at least one underground animal from each of the following types: birds, snakes, amphibians, fish, mammals. Which animals live underground all the time? Which only part of the time?

◆ Imagine that humans lived underground. Make a diagram of an underground home for your family with rooms for sleeping, storage, preparing and eating food, for recreation and spending time together. Don't forget to link the rooms with passages, and draw tunnels for entering and leaving the "home." What systems can you invent for getting around in the dark and for disposing of wastes? How would you keep your underground dwelling safe from intruders?

MORE BOOKS TO READ

Animal Architects. Donald J. Crump, ed. (National Geographic)
Animal Homes. (Dorling Kindersley)
Burrows. Shirley Greenway (Newington)
Dig Hole, Soft Mole. Carolyn Lesser (Harcourt Brace)
Just Mole. C. J. Tripp (Aegine Press)
Platypus. Pauline Reilly (Seven Hills Books)
The Prairie Dog. Dorothy S. Beers (Silver Burdett Press)
The Sierra Club Book of Small Mammals. Linsay Knight (Sierra)
Small Mammals. Anita Ganeri (Franklin Watts)
Towns. Robert Burton (Newington)
What Is a Mammal? Robert Sneddon (Sierra)
The Wind in the Willows. Kenneth Graham (Grosset and Dunlap)

VIDEOS

Mammals: A First Film. (Phoenix/BFA Film and Video)
Platypus. (Centre Communications)
Prairie Dogs: Grassland Survivors. (Altschul Group)
Underground Animals. (Wood Knapp Video)

PLACES TO VISIT

St. Louis Zoological Park
Forest Park
Government Drive
St. Louis, MO 63110

Niagara Falls Museum
5651 River Road
Niagara Falls, Ontario
L2E 6V8

Royal Ontario Museum
110 Queens Park
Toronto, Ontario M5S 2C6

Australian Museum
6-8 College Street
Sydney, NSW
Australia 2000

Museum of Victoria
222 Exhibition Street
Melbourne, Victoria
Australia 3000

San Diego Zoo
Zoo Place and Park
   Boulevard
San Diego, CA 93103

**Auckland Institute and
   Museum**
Auckland Domaine
Auckland, New Zealand

INDEX

Answers to MOLE SECRETS questions:
1. c
2. b
3. c
4. a
5. a
6. b